Contents

Any words appearing in the text in bold, **like this**, are explained in the Glossary.

What is a meadow?

Meadows may be surrounded with hedgerows.

Meadows are areas of land cleared for farming. Farmers may grow plants there to feed their animals. Grasses, shrubs and wild flowers grow in meadows.

Meadows

Louise and Richard Spilsbury

H www.heinemann.co.uk
Visit our website to find out more information about Heinemann Library books.

To order:
☎ Phone 44 (0) 1865 888066
📄 Send a fax to 44 (0) 1865 314091
🖥 Visit the Heinemann Bookshop at www.heinemann.co.uk to browse our catalogue and order online.

First published in Great Britain by Heinemann Library,
Halley Court, Jordan Hill, Oxford OX2 8EJ
a division of Reed Educational and Professional Publishing Ltd.
Heinemann is a registered trademark of Reed Educational & Professional Publishing Ltd.

OXFORD MELBOURNE AUCKLAND JOHANNESBURG BLANTYRE
GABORONE IBADAN PORTSMOUTH (NH) USA CHICAGO

Designed by Celia Floyd
Illustrations by Alan Fraser
Originated by Dot Gradations
Printed in Hong Kong/China

ISBN 0 431 03907 0 (hardback)   ISBN 0 431 03914 3 (paperback)
06 05 04 03 02 01   06 05 04 03 02 01
10 9 8 7 6 5 4 3 2   10 9 8 7 6 5 4 3 2 1

British Library Cataloguing in Publication Data
Spilsbury, Louise
    Meadows. – (Wild Britain)
    1. Meadow ecology – Great Britain – Juvenile literature
    2. Meadow animals – Great Britain – Juvenile literature
    I. Title II. Spilsbury, Richard
    577.4'6

Acknowledgements

To our own young wildlife enthusiasts, Miles and Harriet.

The Publishers would like to thank the following for permission to reproduce photographs:
Bruce Coleman: Hans Reinhard pp7, 27 Andrew Purcell p10, Kim Taylor pp15, 19, 25, George McCarthy p16, Jane Burton pp20, Dennis Green p11, p24; FLPA: Roger Wilmshurst p5; Garden Matters: Ken Gibson p6; Garden & Wildlife Matters: p9; NHPA: David Woodfall pp4, 29, Paal Hermansen p14; Oxford Scientific Films: Ian West p8, Edward Parker p12, G A Maclean p13, G I Bernard p17, 26, Avril Ramage pp18, 21, John Harris p22, Raymond Blythe p23, Muzz Murray p28

Cover photograph reproduced with permission of Images

Our thanks to Andrew Solway for his comments in the preparation of this book.

Every effort has been made to contact copyright holders of any material reproduced in this book. Any omissions will be rectified in subsequent printings if notice is given to the Publisher.

A habitat provides living things, like this marbled white butterfly, with food and **shelter**.

A **habitat** is the natural home of a group of plants and animals. In this book we look at some of the animals and plants that live, grow and **reproduce** in a meadow habitat.

Types of meadow

Farm animals like cows graze on the plants and grasses in some meadows.

In some meadows, farmers grow plants like grass and clover for animals to **graze** on. These meadows are cut by the farmers each year to keep the plants short.

There are many different kinds of plant in this meadow.

Other meadows may not be cut for several years. They are left to grow wild during this time. Many kinds of wild flowers and other plants may grow there.

Changes

The flowers in a meadow attract **insects** like bees and butterflies.

The plants that grow in a meadow change through the year. After the cold, dark winter, spring rain and sunlight help new plants to grow from **seeds**. By summer the meadow is full of flowers.

These meadow grasses have dried during the hot summer.

In autumn the meadow looks quite different. Flowers have gone, leaving **fruit** and seeds on the plants. The grasses have turned brown as they have dried through the hot summer months.

Living there

Mice and voles make long paths through meadow grass, hidden from view.

The meadow **habitat** is quite open so there is little **shelter** for larger animals, like deer. But the tall grass provides shelter for many **insects**, birds and smaller **mammals**.

These goldfinches are feeding on spear thistles.

The insects feed on the plants and dead leaves. Birds and small mammals feed on the insects, as well as some of the plants and their **fruits** and **seeds**.

Grasses

Different types of grass in a meadow have different shaped grass heads.

There are many different types of grass in most meadows. Grasses are thin, tough flowering plants. Grass heads are groups of tiny flowers.

leaf

seed

flower

grass head

stem

Grasses spread quickly because they make lots of seeds.

Grass **seeds** are made in the tiny flowers at the top of the **stems**. The wind blows the seeds off the plants. The seeds land in soil where they may grow into new plants.

Flowering plants

Meadow plants, like this red clover, provide **shelter** and food for many small **insects** and animals.

There are many different meadow flowers. Some are tall, like poppies, buttercups and cornflowers. The red clover is short. Its strong **stem** holds up the flower head.

This orange tip butterfly balances on the forget-me-not flower to drink its sweet nectar.

Many flowering plants need insects to carry their **pollen** from one flower to another, to help them make **seeds**. To attract the insects, flowers have strong scents and make sugary **nectar**.

Butterflies and bumblebees

The marbled white butterfly scatters its eggs in the meadow.

Butterflies lay hundreds of eggs on meadow plants in spring. The caterpillars that **hatch** out of the eggs feed on the leaves of the plants.

Bumblebees feed on flower **nectar** that they lick up with a long tongue.

Many **insects** find **shelter** among meadow plants. Bumblebees live in nests made out of grass and other plants. They often make their nests in old mice holes.

Dung beetles and grasshoppers

Dung beetles help to make piles of dung disappear.

Piles of animal dung in a meadow provide mini **habitats** for dung beetles. They lay their eggs in dung. When the young **hatch** out of the eggs, they eat the dung.

Grasshoppers call to each other by rubbing their legs against their wings.

Grasshoppers feed on the meadow grasses. Their green colour makes them hard to spot. If a bird does try to catch them, they can hop large distances to escape.

Snakes

Grass snakes kill animals they want to eat by biting **poison** into them. Then they swallow them whole.

Snakes are **reptiles**. They need to lie in the sun to get warm. Grass snakes move swiftly through the grass looking for small animals such as mice and frogs to eat.

The old skin is often turned inside out as it comes off.

Female grass snakes **reproduce** by laying soft eggs in rotting leaves. Young snakes **hatch** out of the eggs. As they grow bigger, they grow new skins and **shed** their old skins.

Skylarks and partridges

Skylarks collect grass to build their nests.

All birds **reproduce** by laying eggs in nests. Many meadow birds use grass to make or line their nests. Birds, such as skylarks, build nests among the grasses so they are well hidden.

Grass-like stripes on partridge chicks help to hide them from weasels and foxes that try to eat them.

Partridges lay eggs in hollows in the ground among tall grasses. When the young chicks **hatch** out, they keep still in the grass so they cannot be seen.

Goldfinches and barn owls

Goldfinches pick out thistle seeds using their pointed beaks.

Like all animals, birds need to find food to survive. Goldfinches feed on the **seeds** of teasel and thistle heads and other meadow plants.

A barn owl's wings make little noise so that the animals it catches cannot hear it coming.

The barn owl flies over open meadows at night, listening out for **mammals** like mice or rabbits. It swoops down to catch them in its long, sharp claws, called talons.

Harvest mice and moles

Harvest mice use their nests to sleep in, to keep warm and to bring up babies.

Mammals build or find homes to keep them dry, warm and safe. Harvest mice build nests using strips of torn grass among the meadow plants.

Moles have strong, thick paws. They use them like spades to dig long underground tunnels to live in.

Moles live underground in meadows. Moles cannot see very well. They use their sensitive noses to smell out worms and slugs to eat in the dark.

Dangers

This meadow is being cleared so the farmer can plant **crops** on the land.

Meadows are sometimes cleared to build houses or for farming. The rich mixture of plants is lost when a meadow is cleared.

Spraying pesticides can kill off wild meadow plants.

Overgrazing can also destroy meadows.
This is when farm animals eat away the
plants and they are not replaced. Spraying
land with **pesticides** may also kill the
plants in meadow **habitats**.

Food chains

All plants and animals in a meadow **habitat** are linked through the food they eat. Food chains show how different living things are linked. Here is one example.

The barn owl eats the harvest mouse.

The harvest mouse eats the grasshopper.

The grasshopper feeds on grasses.

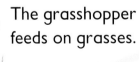

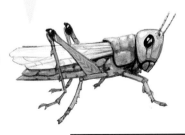

The artwork on this page is not to scale.

Glossary

crops plants that farmers grow to sell as food

fruit part of the plant that holds its seeds

graze eat growing grass

habitat the natural home of a group of plants and animals

hatch to be born from an egg

insects six-legged minibeasts with bodies divided into three sections: head, thorax (chest) and abdomen (stomach)

mammals group of animals that includes humans. All mammals feed their babies with their own milk and have some fur or hair on their bodies.

nectar sweet sugary juice in the centre of a flower

pesticides sprays farmers use to kill insects that damage crops

poison chemical that can damage or kill living things

pollen tiny yellow specks that make seeds which grow into another flower

reproduce when plants and animals make young just like themselves

reptiles scaly animals such as lizards and snakes. Reptiles are cold-blooded, meaning their body temperature changes depending on where they are.

seeds these are made by a plant and released to grow into new plants

shed let or make something fall off

shelter somewhere safe to stay, live and have young

stem the stalk that holds up the leaves, flowers and fruit of a plant

Index